NATURE ⌕ WATCH
COBRAS

Written by
Sylvia A. Johnson

Lerner Publications Company • Minneapolis

CONTENTS

The author wishes to thank Wolfgang Wüster, Lecturer in Zoology, School of Biology, University of Wales, for his assistance in the preparation of this book.

Text copyright © 2007 by Sylvia A. Johnson

Lerner Publications Company
A division of Lerner Publishing Group
241 First Avenue North
Minneapolis, MN 55401 U.S.A.

Website address: www.lernerbooks.com

Library of Congress Cataloging-in-Publication Data

Johnson, Sylvia A.
    Cobras / by Sylvia A. Johnson.
      p.   cm. — (Nature watch)
    Includes bibliographical references and index.
    ISBN-13: 978–1–57505–871–9 (lib. bdg. : alk. paper)
    ISBN-10: 1–57505–871–5 (lib. bdg. : alk. paper)
    1. Cobras—Juvenile literature. I. Title. II. Series: Nature
watch (Minneapolis, Minn.)
    QL666.O64J64 2007
    597.96'42—dc22   2006008151

Manufactured in the United States of America
1 2 3 4 5 6 – DP – 12 11 10 09 08 07

Cobras, like this Indian spectacled cobra, are feared and respected by people all over the world.

WHAT IS A COBRA?

WHEN MOST PEOPLE THINK OF COBRAS, THEY PICTURE A
large snake rising out of a basket, accompanied by the haunting music of
a flute. Or maybe they imagine a snake spraying **venom** straight into the
face of an attacker. These images of cobras are not wrong, but they are
only a small part of the story of these fascinating snakes.

Cobras are not found in North and South America or in Europe, but
they are common in Africa and in many parts of Asia. Wherever they
live, the snakes seem to arouse extreme reactions in humans. Feared and
hated by many, cobras are also honored and respected. Why do people
see cobras in such different ways? What are these snakes of story and
legend really like?

What is a cobra? This may sound like a simple question, but the answer is not so simple. Many snakes have the common name cobra. To mention only a few, there is the Egyptian cobra, the Indian cobra, the Chinese cobra, the king cobra, and the forest cobra. There are also spitting cobras, tree cobras, and water cobras. To understand how all these snakes are related and which ones are entitled to the name cobra, you need to know something about scientific **classification.**

COBRA GROUPS

Classification is a system used by scientists who study animals and plants. It is a way to show relationships among living things by arranging them in groups. Animals in the same group are more or less alike, with similar physical features. The smaller the group, the more its members have in common.

Cobras, like all snakes, are **reptiles,** members of the scientific class Reptilia. Reptiles are cold-blooded animals, which means that their body temperatures are controlled by their surroundings. Warm-blooded animals such as birds and mammals are able to control their body temperature.

Scientists divide reptiles into several orders, and one is Squamata, which includes snakes and lizards. Snakes have

The Indian spectacled cobra is just one of many kinds of cobras.

SCIENTIFIC CLASSIFICATION OF THE CAPE COBRA

PHYLUM	Chordata (animals with backbones
CLASS	Reptilia (reptiles)
ORDER	Squamata (snakes and lizards)
SUBORDER	Serpentes (snakes)
FAMILY	Elapidae (venomous snakes found in warm regions of Africa, Asia, Australia, and North and South America)
GENUS	*Naja*
SPECIES	*Naja nivea* (Cape cobra)

their own suborder, called Serpentes. The next group in the system of classification is family. Snakes are divided into 18 different families, some small and others very large.

All the cobras mentioned earlier are members of a large family called Elapidae. **Elapids** (eh-LA-pids) live in many parts of the world and can be very different in appearance. One thing that they all have in common is venom, or poison. All elapid snakes, including the cobras, are venomous.

In the system of classification, families are divided into smaller groups, each of which is known as a **genus** (GEE-nus). The family Elapidae is made up of about 62 genera (the Latin plural of genus.) Most of the snakes that scientists think of as cobras belong to a genus named *Naja* (NAH-juh or NAH-yuh).

7

A genus is divided into even smaller groups called **species**. Each species is made up of animals that have many physical characteristics in common. In determining species, scientists look at such things as bone structure and number of teeth. One feature used in classifying snakes is the pattern of the scales on their heads and bodies. Members of a species have similar genes (the units of heredity) and common ancestors.

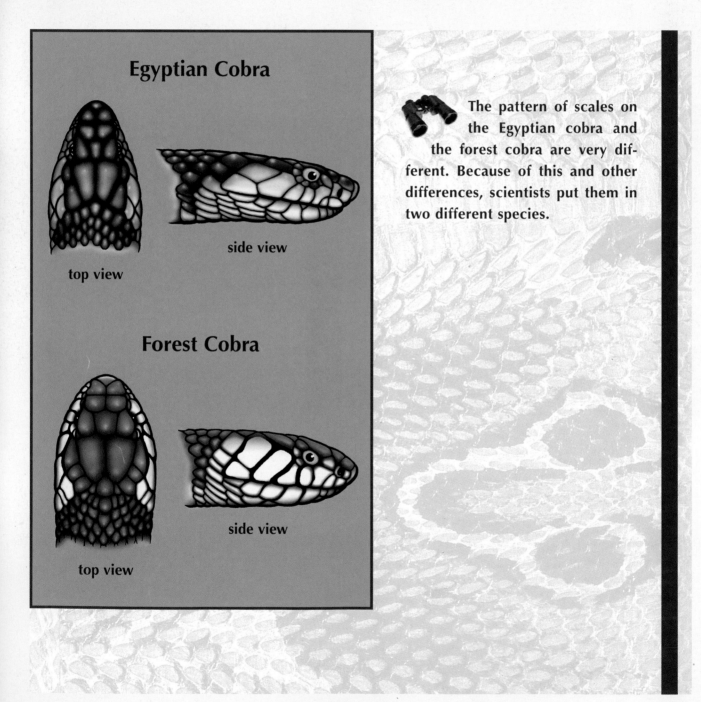

Egyptian Cobra

side view

top view

Forest Cobra

side view

top view

The pattern of scales on the Egyptian cobra and the forest cobra are very different. Because of this and other differences, scientists put them in two different species.

The scientific name for these Malayan spitting cobras is *Naja sputatrix*. *Sputatrix* means they spit.

There are 20 known species of cobras in the genus *Naja*, 9 in Africa and 11 in Asia. Each one has a Latin name that is used by scientists all over the world, no matter what language they speak. The Egyptian cobra, for example, is called *Naja haje*. The red spitting cobra is *Naja pallida*. (As you can see, a species name always includes the name of the genus.) A snake may have several different common names, even in a single language, but it has only one scientific name.

The 20 *Naja* species are considered "typical" or "true" cobras by many **herpetologists** (her-peh-TAHL-uh-jists). These scientists study reptiles and amphibians (frogs and salamanders). Most of the spitting cobras are included in this group, but the water and tree cobras are not. The king cobra is also not a typical cobra. This snake lives in the same regions as some of the *Naja* cobras, however, and is often grouped with them.

Though it isn't a true cobra, the king cobra lives in the same areas as many true cobras.

TYPICAL COBRAS

THE *NAJA* COBRAS LIVE IN MANY PARTS OF AFRICA AND Asia, usually in warm regions. They can be found in countries such as Egypt, Tanzania, Namibia, South Africa, India, Pakistan, Thailand, Cambodia, and the Philippine Islands, just to name a few.

Throughout their range, cobras live in different kinds of environments. In Africa the Egyptian cobra makes its home in dry, semidesert regions as well as in grasslands. Another African species, the forest cobra *(Naja melanoleuca)*, inhabits forested areas and is good at climbing trees. The red spitting cobra *(Naja pallida)*, shown above, is often found in dry areas near rivers or in places where there are springs and wells in the desert.

Cobras in Asia also live in a variety of environments. The Central Asian cobra *(Naja oxiana)* inhabits dry regions in Pakistan, Iran, and Afghanistan. The Chinese cobra *(Naja atra)* and the Indian spectacled cobra *(Naja naja)* are common in grasslands and near fields of cultivated rice. The Indonesian spitting cobra *(Naja siamensis)*, found in Thailand, Cambodia, and parts of Laos and Vietnam, also lives near rice fields.

Many cobra species in Asia and Africa make their homes near or in villages, towns, and even cities. The Indian spectacled cobra and the monocled cobra *(Naja kaouthia)* live in or near cities in many parts of Asia. In northern Africa, people in the heavily populated Nile River valley may have Egyptian cobras as close neighbors.

The golden cape cobra lives in South Africa.

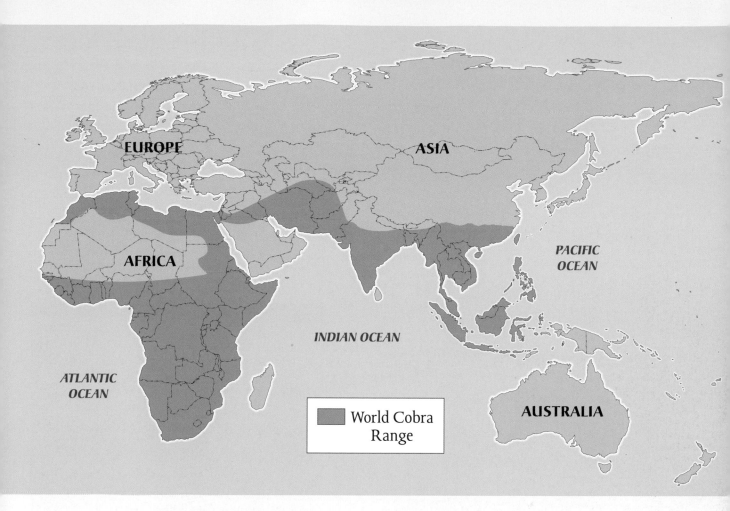

Map labels:
EUROPE
ASIA
AFRICA
PACIFIC OCEAN
INDIAN OCEAN
ATLANTIC OCEAN
AUSTRALIA

World Cobra Range

Naja cobras not only live in different environments but they can also look very different. Depending on the species, cobras can vary greatly in size. The Indonesian spitting cobra and the southeastern Philippine cobra *(Naja samarensis)* average 3 to 4 feet (about 1 m) long. The Egyptian cobra and the forest cobra may be more than 7 feet (2 m) long. Most *Naja* cobras are shades of yellow, tan, brown, or black, with markings such as stripes, spots, and bands. Even cobras within a single species often vary in appearance. In some species, young cobras also have different colors and markings than he adults do.

A COBRA'S HOOD

Despite these differences, cobras have some obvious features in common. One of these is the cobra's **hood**. This is an area of skin that spreads out around the snake's neck. Photographs of cobras usually show the hood. But if you saw a cobra resting in the sun or moving silently along a path, its hood would not be visible. It appears only when the snake needs to defend itself against an attacker.

13

Cobras, like all snakes, are **predators** that kill animals for food. But they are also **prey** and are killed and eaten by other predators. Among the animals that hunt cobras are large birds such as eagles and secretary birds, mammals such as the mongoose, and even other snakes.

When threatened by a predator, a cobra raises the upper third of its body off the ground into an upright position. Then it spreads its hood. It uses long, flexible ribs in the neck region to stretch out the skin, something like opening an umbrella. The hood makes the cobra look bigger and threatening to an attacker. By raising up the front part of its body and spreading its hood, a cobra sends the message that it is big and strong and ready to fight. This alone may be enough to scare a predator away.

Inset: Sensing danger, a cobra rises up and spreads its hood.
Above: A yellow cobra has become a meal for a goshawk in Africa's Kalahari Desert.

When the Indian spectacled cobra spreads its hood, it displays markings on the back of its head. The markings look something like a pair of old-fashioned spectacles, or eyeglasses. Other Asian species such as the Chinese cobra have similar markings. A cobra's hood with its "spectacles" is a warning sign to predators. The monocled cobra, found

Left: The Indian spectacled cobra is named for the markings on its hood.
Below: The monocled cobra has only one eye spot on its hood.

in India and other countries of South Asia, has a single eye-shaped mark on its head. This mark, like the Indian cobra's spectacles, may actually look like the eye of a large animal to its enemies. Even when the cobra is moving away, it still seems to be watching for an attack.

If a cobra's hood and markings do not scare away a predator, then it has another powerful weapon—venom. All the *Naja* cobras use venom both to defend themselves and to get food. Venom is a very important part of their way of life.

All *Naja* cobras have hoods, but they are not all the same size. The Indian spectacled cobra, the Egyptian cobra, and the monocled cobra have large, broad hoods. The hoods of many spitting cobras are small and narrow.

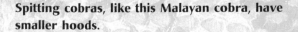
Spitting cobras, like this Malayan cobra, have smaller hoods.

A Cobra's Venom

MANY PEOPLE HAVE A SPECIAL INTEREST IN VENOMOUS snakes. They fear them but are also fascinated by the snakes' use of deadly poisons. Of the more than 3,000 species of snakes in the world, only about 375 are venomous. All members of the family Elapidae carry venom. Another family, Viperidae, is also made up entirely of venomous species. This family, the **vipers,** includes rattlesnakes and the pit viper, shown above.

Herpetologists often divide venomous snakes into groups based on their **fangs**, the special teeth used to carry the venom. Cobras and other elapids belong to a group of snakes with short fangs in the front of their mouths. These fangs are fixed in position—they don't move.

Vipers also have front fangs, but they are hinged rather than fixed. When a rattlesnake or other viper closes its mouth, its long fangs fold back against the roof of the mouth. A third group of snakes, the colubrid snakes, has fangs in the rear of the mouth. The very venomous African boomslang belongs to this group.

There are some other differences in the fangs of venomous snakes. The fangs of elapids and vipers are hollow. Venom runs through the center of the fang to an opening at the bottom. The fangs of rear-fanged snakes are not hollow but have grooves in the surface. The venom runs through these grooves.

Colubrid snakes, like this African boomslang, have fangs in the rear of their mouths.

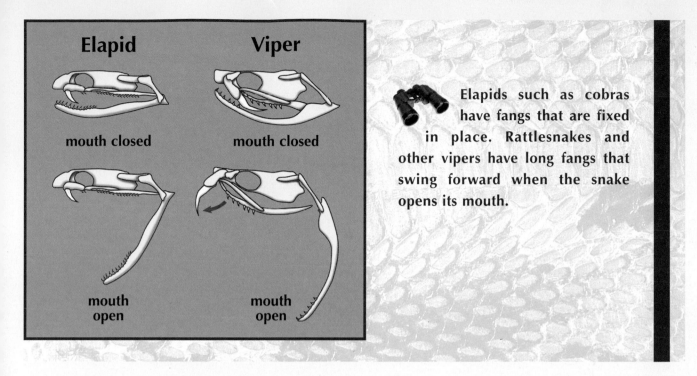

Elapid   **Viper**

mouth closed   mouth closed

mouth open   mouth open

Elapids such as cobras have fangs that are fixed in place. Rattlesnakes and other vipers have long fangs that swing forward when the snake opens its mouth.

ABOUT VENOM

Snake venom is a very complicated substance. It is a kind of saliva produced in glands (special organs) inside a snake's head. Small tubes carry it to the fangs. Venom contains different chemicals that affect the bodies of animals in different ways. The venom of cobras and other elapids, for example, includes chemicals that affect the brain, spinal chord, and nerves. This kind of venom is often described as **neurotoxic**. Viper venom usually attacks the blood. Herpetologists call this kind of venom **hemotoxic**.

New scientific research shows that venom can't be divided so neatly into these two groups. Although most cobra venom is mainly neurotoxic, it may also contain a mix of other chemicals. Herpetologists are studying the venom of cobras and other snakes to learn more about these complicated substances.

Whatever its makeup, a snake's venom has one main purpose—to injure or kill other animals. Like all venomous snakes, cobras use their venom in self-defense if they have no other choice. If a monocled cobra can't frighten an attacker away by displaying its hood and its eye marking, it may strike out and try to sink its fangs into the enemy.

Cobras don't always inject venom when they bite. Snakes can control the flow of venom from the venom glands. They can change the amount or even cut off the flow completely. When it comes to self-defense, a bite alone may be enough to discourage an attacker. Sometimes even a bite is unnecessary. Some cobras just butt their heads against an enemy to drive it away.

The spitting cobras don't have to bite at all. They can spray venom through their fangs at an enemy. Spitting cobras use strong muscles surrounding the venom glands to force venom out of the small openings in their fangs. The action is something like shooting water from a water pistol. If the venom hits an animal's skin, it does little damage. But if it gets into the eyes, it causes intense pain and temporary blindness, allowing the cobra to glide away to safety.

Six species of *Naja* cobras in Asia and five in Africa are definitely known to spray venom. Some *Naja* cobras have fangs like those of spitting cobras, but they rarely spit venom. The monocled cobra and the Chinese cobra belong to this group.

Scientific studies have shown that spitting cobras seem to defend themselves more actively against attackers than the non-spitting species. Spitters can spray venom from a safe distance, as much as 12 feet (3.5 m) away. Their non-spitting relatives have to get up close in order to bite. Escape might be a better choice for these cobras.

HUNTING PREY

Venom is used in self-defense, but its main purpose is to obtain food. In killing prey animals for food, predators such as lions and grizzly bears use their powerful claws and teeth. Snakes have no claws. Their teeth are not suitable for killing or tearing up prey. They have a different way of getting their food. Venomous snakes use their venom to kill their prey.

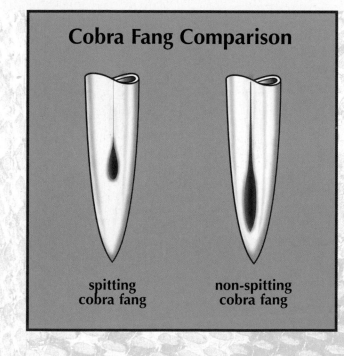

Cobra Fang Comparison

spitting
cobra fang

non-spitting
cobra fang

Spitting cobras have fangs especially adapted for spitting. The openings in the fangs that release venom are smaller and more rounded than those of non-spitting species. They are also located farther away from the tip of the fang.

Right: A cobra will first try to frighten an enemy by displaying its hood.

Below: This Mozambique spitting cobra sprays two jets of venom at its attacker's eyes.

An Asian cobra uses its forked tongue to collect scents and find prey.

All snakes are hunters. They wait in hiding or track prey with their keen sense of smell. Snakes have nostrils, but they mainly use their forked tongues to pick up odors. As it hunts, a snake rapidly darts its tongue in and out. The tongue collects scent particles from the air and the ground and brings them back inside the snake's mouth. In the roof of the mouth are two small cavities called the **Jacobson's organ**. When the snake inserts the tips of its tongue into these cavities, the Jacobson's organ analyzes the scent particles and sends a message to the snake's brain. If the snake is lucky, the message says that a prey animal is near.

When snakes capture their prey, they swallow it whole. They use their flexible jaws and sharp, curved teeth to pull prey animals into their throats, usually head first. Saliva in a snake's throat starts the digestion process at once. Digestion is completed after the prey reaches the snake's stomach.

Snakes sometimes swallow small prey animals alive, but larger animals have to be killed first. Venomous snakes use their poison to kill prey.

Rattlesnakes and other vipers usually strike prey quickly and then let go.

Cobras and other elapids bite and hold on, chewing on the prey animal to force venom into its body.

Cobras strike from a slightly raised position. They do not rise up and spread their hoods when killing for food. Like all cobras, spitting cobras kill their prey by biting. Spitting is used only in self-defense.

All snakes have flexible jaws and can swallow prey whole. This Indian spectacled cobra is eating a rodent.

The venom of most cobras affects the nervous system. It prevents the prey animal from moving and eventually stops it from breathing. Viper venom usually attacks the blood. When any type of venom is injected into the prey's body, it immediately starts the process of digestion, even before the snake begins to swallow its meal.

Since the *Naja* cobras of Africa and Asia live in many different environments, their prey is quite varied. It includes rats, mice, frogs, toads, lizards, birds and bird eggs, and small mammals.

The king cobra usually eats other snakes, including other cobras. In fact, its genus name, *Ophiophagus*, means "snake eater." Some other cobras eat snakes too.

King cobras are the longest of all the venomous snakes, sometimes reaching 18 feet (5 m) in length. Their venom is powerful, and they can inject large amounts of it. There have been reports of a king cobra biting an elephant on the foot and injecting enough venom to kill it. King cobras live in many countries of Asia, including India, but are not often seen by humans.

King cobras eat other snakes.

Many nonvenomous snakes also hunt and kill prey. When a nonvenomous snake catches a small animal, it may grab the prey and begin swallowing while the animal is still alive. Larger prey has to be killed before it is eaten. Snakes such as boas and pythons use constriction to kill their prey. These snakes wrap their bodies around a prey animal and squeeze until the prey is unable to breathe.

The emerald tree boa and other boas squeeze their prey to kill it.

PRODUCING YOUNG

ALL ANIMALS NEED TO DEFEND THEMSELVES FROM ATTACK and find food. A third important need is reproduction. The way most cobras produce young is similar to reproduction in other snakes.

Snakes are solitary animals, living alone most of their lives. At mating time, males usually find female partners by using their sense of smell. Sometimes two males will find the same female and fight to mate with her. Male forest cobras in Africa have these kinds of battles and so do king cobras. Two males will twist their muscular bodies together and wrestle back and forth. These fights don't usually end in injury or death. One male eventually gives up and goes to look for another mate.

After mating, pairs of *Naja* cobras do not usually stay together. The male and female go back to their solitary lives, and the female gets ready to have her young.

Cobras, like many other female snakes, reproduce by laying eggs. Scientists call these snakes **oviparous** (oh-VIP-uh-rus). Other kinds of snakes are **viviparous** (vih-VIP-uh-rus)—the young come out of the mother's body alive, Almost all the elapids of Asia and Africa are egg layers. Many elapids in Australia give birth to live young. So do other snakes such as boas, garter snakes, and rattlesnakes.

A female cobra lays long, oval eggs.

LAYING EGGS

When female cobras are ready to lay their eggs, they usually look for damp areas in rock crevices or hollow logs or under piles of brush or leaves. Cobras in Africa and some parts of Asia may lay their eggs in the tunnels of termite mounds. In such places, the eggs can stay warm, moist, and protected.

After most female snakes lay their eggs, they leave and never return. This is true of some cobras, but not all. The females of some Asian *Naja* species, for example, the Indian spectacled cobra and the monocled cobra, are known to stay near their eggs after laying them. Scientists believe that the snakes are guarding the eggs from predators.

Left: Indian spectacled cobras stay near their eggs. They may be protecting them from predators.
Below: A baby Sri Lankan cobra glides past empty egg shells.

This young king cobra may have had as many as 40 nest mates.

The female king cobra makes a kind of nest for her eggs. Using a loop of her body, she collects vegetation and soil and puts them in a pile. After laying the eggs in the pile, she coils on top of the nest or stays nearby to guard it. By lying on top of the nest, a female king cobra may provide some warmth to help in the eggs' development. Herpetologists believe that the female's mate some- times stays near the nest to help protect the eggs.

How many eggs do *Naja* cobras lay? This is not an easy question to answer because scientists do not have much information about the lives of some species. We know that the king cobra usually lays about 20 to 40 eggs at one time. The Indian spectacled cobra lays about 12 to 30 eggs. The Egyptian cobra

A baby Chinese cobra crawls out of its egg, while another baby nearby uses its egg tooth to cut through the leathery shell.

lays 15 to 20. The monocled cobra lays about 10 to 20. The length of time before the eggs hatch varies depending on the species and also on outside conditions such as warmth and moisture. The eggs of an Indian spectacled cobra usually hatch 50 to 60 days after they are laid. The eggs of the monocled cobra may take as long as 80 days to hatch.

HATCHING

When it is time for hatching, a young cobra uses a special **egg tooth** to cut through the leathery eggshell. This is not really a tooth but a small projection on the upper jaw. It falls off after hatching is complete. As soon as young cobras leave their eggs, they are ready to take care of themselves. They have venom in their glands, and they know how to use it. At the beginning of their lives, the young snakes are usually not large enough to hunt the same prey animals that their parents do. Until they get bigger, they may eat smaller animals such as frogs and toads.

Most cobras are able to reproduce when they are three or four years old. Scientists don't have much information about how long the snakes live in the wild. In captivity, the monocled cobra may live for more than 12 years. Records show that Indian spectacled cobras can reach the age of 17.

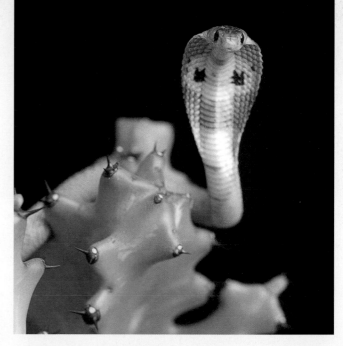

A baby cobra hides behind a cactus.

 As they grow, all snakes shed the outer layer of their skins. Under the old skin is a new layer that will be shed when the snake gets bigger. A young cobra usually sheds its skin during the first week after hatching. It will continue growing and shedding throughout its life or until it reaches full size for its species.

COBRAS AND
PEOPLE

WHEN PEOPLE IN ANCIENT TIMES SAW SNAKES SHEDDING
their skins and emerging with shiny new scales, they were impressed and
awed. Many came to view snakes as symbols of rebirth and new life. In
the modern world, snakes—particularly cobras—still inspire strong
beliefs and feelings in humans.

One of the most common human responses to cobras is fear. Even
people who live in regions where there are no cobras are terrified by the
idea of the snakes' venomous bite.

Of course, we know that cobras do not go around looking for people to bite and kill. Humans are too large to be a cobra's prey. If a *Naja* cobra bites a person, it is in self-defense, usually after snake and human have crossed paths accidentally. This happens most often in places where cobras and people live close together. Cobra species such as the Indian spectacled cobra and the monocled cobra are common in heavily populated regions of Asia. In these areas, people even find cobras inside their houses, where the snakes have come seeking water or shade.

Cobra bites may be common, but they are not always fatal. Many things affect the deadliness of a cobra's bite. These include the general health of the victim, the location of the bite, and especially the amount of venom delivered. A victim treated with cobra **antivenin** usually has a good chance of surviving.

Boys in Zimbabwe carry a cobra they found in their garden.

ANTIVENINS

Antivenin acts against the damaging effects of a bite. This medicine is produced from venom taken from live snakes. Some antivenins are made from the venom of only one species. Others are made from a mix of venoms.

Hospitals and clinics have a supply of antivenins that are effective against the most common venomous snakes in their particular region.

If a victim has received a large dose of venom and no antivenin is available, a cobra bite may be deadly. Symptoms

Right: **This packet contains cobra antivenin collected for use in Thailand.**
Below: **This mix of a number of different antivenins is for use in South Africa.**

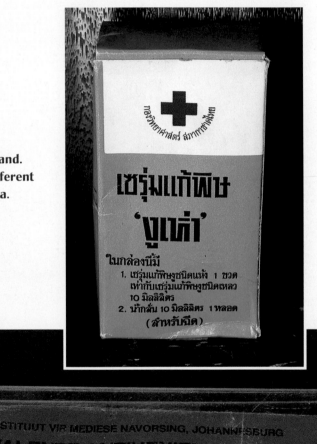

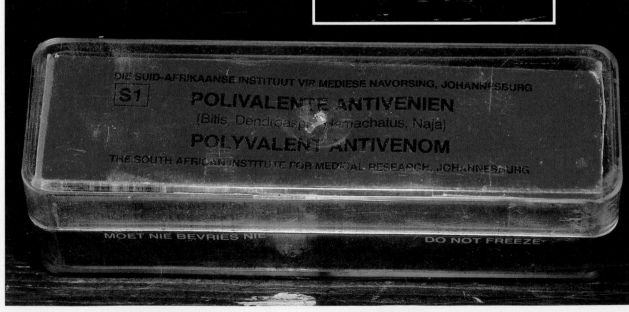

34

A spectacled cobra is milked for its venom.

vary depending on the species of cobra, but there are some common signs. At first, the person may feel intense pain in the area of the bite. Paralysis starts in the face and gradually spreads to the rest of the body. The victim has increasing difficulty breathing and eventually dies.

Millions of people in Asia and Africa live in areas where cobras are common. They fear the venomous snakes, but many also believe that cobras have special powers that can be used to help humans.

It has been estimated that in India alone, at least 10,000 people die from cobra bites every year. However, because snakebites are often not reported, accurate numbers are not available.

35

Ancient Egyptian pharaohs wore crowns with the figure of a cobra in the front.

COBRAS IN RELIGION

For thousands of years, cobras have had a special place in religious beliefs. The ancient Egyptians worshipped a cobra goddess. The image of a cobra with spread hood appeared on the crown worn by their Eyptian rulers, the powerful pharaohs. A real cobra is reported to have played a role in Egyptian history. When the ruler Cleopatra took her own life by letting a snake bite her, the snake was probably an Egyptian cobra.

In Bangalore, India, an Indian woman and her grandchild sit by cobra images at a Hindu temple.

Cobras have also been important in Hinduism, a religion that originated in India and is still practiced by millions of people. In ancient times, snake gods called nagas were worshipped in India. (The scientific name *Naja* comes from *naga*, a word in the ancient Sanskrit language of India.) Nagas appeared to humans in the form of cobras. They often helped people by making their lands fertile and giving them children. But they could also punish those who did not honor them and offer them gifts. In modern India, the nagas are still worshipped in village shrines and temples.

Many Indians not only pray to cobra gods but also consider it good luck if a real cobra makes its home in the gardens or courtyards of their houses. They put out food for the snake and ask it to protect their homes and families.

These cobra figures are used in an Indian snake festival.

Cobras are linked to another important Asian religion, Buddhism. The founder of this ancient religion was an Indian prince named Siddhartha Gautama, later known as the Buddha. Stories tell that nagas were present when the prince was born. It is said that a great naga king once spread his hood over the Buddha to protect him from the sun. In gratitude, the Buddha kissed the snake on the back of the head. His kiss left the round mark that can still be seen on the heads of monocled cobras.

This Cambodian statue of the Buddha shows him sitting on a cobra and being sheltered by its hood.

An Indian snake charmer lures two cobras from their baskets.

Another kind of relationship between cobras and humans can be seen in the performances of snake charmers. They are almost always men. Snake charmers work in villages, towns, and cities in northern Africa, India, and other Asian countries. The snake charmer sits on the ground before a covered basket, playing a flute. When the cover is removed, a large cobra (usually an Indian spectacled cobra or an Egyptian cobra) rises up out of the basket. The snake spreads its hood and seems to sway to the music of the flute.

A snake charmer removes a cobra's fangs to protect himself from being bitten.

A snake charmer's perfomance is based on the natural behavior of cobras. All cobras rise up and spread their hoods when they are frightened or alarmed. The cobra's swaying has little to do with the music being played. Snakes don't have ears on the outsides of their bodies. They can't hear sounds in the way that humans and other animals do. They can only feel the sound vibrations. The cobra is swaying because it sees the snake charmer mov-

ing his body back and forth as he plays the flute. Alert to the man's movements, the cobra is waiting for a chance to defend itself.

If the cobra tries to attack the human, it doesn't have much of a chance. Snake charmers know that a cobra can strike out only as far as its body is raised off the ground. They sit far enough away from the basket so that the cobras can't reach them. Some snake charmers even pull out their snakes' fangs or sew up their mouths to prevent any possibility of injury. When the cobra dies of starvation or infection, the snake charmer just goes out and catches another one.

THE FUTURE FOR COBRAS

In some parts of Asia, snake charming is not as common as it once was. India, for example, has passed wildlife protection laws that make it illegal for people to keep wild snakes. Under these laws, snake charmers may be arrested for having cobras and performing with them.

Although cobras may be less likely to end up in a snake charmer's basket, other dangers threaten them. Like wild animals in many parts of the world, some cobras are losing their natural homes to human development. This is especially true in heavily populated parts of Asia such as India and China.

Cobras in Asia face other threats caused by human actions. Many of the cobras of Asia are being killed and sold for human use. In countries such as Indonesia, cobras are killed for their skins, which are used to make belts, shoes, and purses.

This cobra-skin purse was taken by a government agency. Trade in cobra skins is illegal in many countries.

Merchants offer cobra meat for sale at a market in South Vietnam.
Inset: **Bottles with cobras preserved in liquid are sold as cobra wine in Vietnam and other places in Asia.**

People in many parts of Asia eat cobra meat. In southern China, for example, snake meat is a very common item on the menu. Every day food markets in Chinese towns sell thousands of wild cobras and other snakes for the cooking pot.

In countries such as Vietnam, cobras are used to make traditional medicines. Cobra blood and cobra "wine" (liquid in which cobra bodies have been preserved) are also highly valued in some parts of Asia.

The Convention on International Trade in Endangered Species (CITES) is a group that regulates trade in wild animals and plants. It has put all Asian *Naja* species on a danger list. The countries that belong to the CITES group are trying to control the buying and selling of cobras in Asia. They have set up rules about trading cobra skins and other cobra products, but these rules are not always followed by the member countries. If the efforts of CITES and similar organizations do not succeed, cobras in Asia may face a bleak future. **Extinction** for some species is a real possibility.

Perhaps you think that the disappearance of Asian cobras might not be such a bad thing. Cobras are venomous snakes that can be a threat to humans. Who needs them? But the extinction of any animal or plant species can change the world in ways we cannot predict. In some areas of Asia, overhunting of cobras and other snakes may have already led to increased numbers of rodents, which destroy crops and carry disease.

Our world could very well be a more dangerous place without cobras in it. It would certainly be less interesting.

In bright sunlight, an Indian spectacled cobra is a colorful sight. Like all animals, cobras have a place in the natural world.

GLOSSARY

antivenin: a medicine made of snake venom that acts against the effect of a snakebite

classification: a scientific system used to study relationships among living things. In classification, animals and plants are placed into groups based on their similar characteristics. The smaller the group, the more its members have in common.

egg tooth: a bony projection on a young snake's upper jaw. It is used to cut through the eggshell at hatching.

elapids: members of the family Elapidae. Cobras, coral snakes, and mambas are elapids.

extinction: when a kind of animal is gone forever

fangs: the special teeth that venomous snakes use to deliver venom

genus: a group in the system of classification that is part of a family. Typical cobras belong to the family Elapidae and the genus *Naja*.

hemotoxic: poisonous to the blood. The venom of rattlesnakes and other vipers is mainly hemotoxic.

herpetologists: scientists who study reptiles (snakes, lizards, turtles, and crocodiles) and amphibians (frogs, toads, and salamanders)

hood: an area of skin around the cobra's head. A cobra spreads its hood in self-defense.

Jacobson's organ: an organ in a snake's head made up of two sacs lined with nerve endings that are sensitive to odors

neurotoxic: poisonous to the nervous system. Cobra venom is mainly neurotoxic.

oviparous: producing young that hatch from eggs. All cobras are oviparous.

predators: animals that kill and eat other animals

prey: animals that are killed and eaten by other animals

reptiles: animals that belong to the scientific class Reptilia. Reptiles are cold-blooded animals. Their temperatures are controlled by their surroundings. Snakes, lizards, turtles, crocodiles, and alligators are all reptiles.

species: a group in the system of classification with many features in common. A genus is divided into two or more species.

venom: poison used by snakes to defend themselves and to get food

vipers: a family of venomous snakes that includes rattlesnakes

viviparous: producing live young, rather than laying eggs

SELECTED BIBLIOGRAPHY

Convention on International Trade in Endangered Species.
   http://www.cites.org

Greene, Harry W. *Snakes: The Evolution of Mystery in Nature.* Berkeley: University of
   California Press, 1997.

Huyler, Stephen R. *Meeting God: Elements of Hindu Devotion.* New Haven, CT: Yale
   University Press, 1999.

Marais, Johan. *A Complete Guide to the Snakes of Southern Africa.* Malabar, FL:
   Krieger, 1992.

Mattison, Chris. *The Encyclopedia of Snakes.* New York: Facts on Files, 1995.

————. *Snakes of the World.* New York: Facts on File, 1986.

Minton, Sherman and Madge Rutherford Minton. *Venomous Reptiles.* Rev. ed. New
   York: Scribner, 1980.

O'Shea, Mark. *Venomous Snakes of the World.* Princeton, NJ: Princeton University
   Press, 2005.

Riccuiti, Edward R. *The Snake Almanac: A Fully Illustrated Natural History of Snakes
   Worldwide.* New York: Lyons Press, 2001.

Spawls, Stephen, and Bill Branch. *The Dangerous Snakes of Africa.* Sanibel Island, FL:
   Ralph Curtis Books, 1995.

Wüster, Wolfgang. "The Asiatic Cobra Systematics Page." *Wolfgang Wüster.*
   http://biology.bangor.ac.uk/~bss166/Taxa/AsNaja.htm

WEBSITES

"King Cobra." *National Geographic.*

    http://www.nationalgeographic.com/animals/reptiles/king-cobra.html

    An article, photos, factsheet, and video about the king cobra are available on this site.

Klein, John A. "Cobra." *Cobra Information Site.*

    http://www.cobras.org

    This site has text, photos, maps, diagrams, and even audio—all about cobras.

Simon, Tamar. "The Truth behind Snake Charming." *Discovery Channel.*

    http://www.exn.ca/snakes/story.asp?id=1999090854.

    This discussion of snake charmers gives the true story of what the snake charmers are really doing and of how the snakes are treated.

FURTHER READING

Gerholdt, James E. *King Cobras.* Edina, MN: Abdo & Daughters, 1996.

McCarthy, Colin. *Reptile.* New York: Dorling Kindersley, 2000

Schnieper, Claudia. *Snakes.* Minneapolis: Carolrhoda Books, Inc., 1995.

Stone, Lynn M. *Snakes with Venom.* Vero Beach, FL: Rourke Books Co., 2001.

INDEX

ABOUT THE AUTHOR

Sylvia A. Johnson has had a long and productive career as an editor and writer of award-winning books for young people. She has worked on publications about such different subjects as beekeeping, raptor rehabilitation, and the role of maps in history. Doing research for her books, Sylvia has studied rare old maps in libraries, observed surgery on injured raptors, and put on overalls and a veiled hat to get a close-up look at a beekeeper at work. For her book on American crows, she studied the birds in her own backyard in Minneapolis, Minnesota. When she is not doing research for books, Sylvia enjoys reading, working in the garden, cooking Indian food, and traveling to Mexico and Central America to visit the ruins of ancient Mayan cities.

PHOTO ACKNOWLEDGEMENTS

The images in this book are used with the permission of: © Allen Blake Sheldon, pp. 2-3, 6, 11, 15 (both), 41 and all backgrounds on pp. 1, 5, 7, 8, 11, 16, 17, 19, 20, 25, 26, 31, 32, 35, 44, 45, 46, 47, 48; © Claudia Adams/Root Resources, p. 4; © Michael & Patricia Fogden/CORBIS, p. 5; © Getty Images, pp. 7, 21 (bottom), 33, 37 (top); © Laura Westlund/Independent Picture Service, pp. 8, 13, 19, 20; © Dan Nedrelo, pp. 9, 16; © Photocyclops.com/ SuperStock, p. 10; © Joe McDonald/CORBIS, pp. 12, 14 (right), 31 (left); © Clem Haagner; Gallo Images/CORBIS, p. 14 (left); © Ken Lucas/Visuals Unlimited, p. 17; © Chris Mattison, p. 18; © David Fleetham/Alamy, p. 21 (top); © H. Stanley Johnson/SuperStock, p. 22; © Joe McDonald/Visuals Unlimited, pp. 25, 26; © Jim Merli/Visuals Unlimited, p. 27; © age fotostock/SuperStock, pp. 28 (top), 37 (bottom), 42, 43; © Anuruddha Lokuhapuarachchi/ Reuters/Corbis, p. 28 (bottom); © McDonald, Joe/Animals Animals, p. 29; © Bruce Coleman Inc./Alamy, p. 30; © DPA/TSS/The Image Works, p. 31 (right); © Reuters/CORBIS, p. 32; © James E. Gerholdt, p. 34 (both); © Michael & Patricia Fogden/Minden Pictures, p. 35; © Archivo Iconografico, S.A/CORBIS, p. 36; © SuperStock, Inc./SuperStock, p. 38; © John R. Kreul/Independent Picture Service, p. 39; © Jeffrey L. Rotman/CORBIS, p. 40; © Michael Freeman/CORBIS, p. 42 (inset).

Front Cover: © David A. Northcott/CORBIS.

Back Cover: © Allen Blake Sheldon.